W9-CKT-529

LIFE IN THE FAST LANE

INSIDE A
SPRINT CAR

H. PHILLIPS

Cavendish
Square

New York

Published in 2015 by Cavendish Square Publishing, LLC
243 5th Avenue, Suite 136, New York, NY 10016

Copyright © 2015 by Cavendish Square Publishing, LLC

First Edition

This publication represents the opinions and views of the author based on his or her personal experience, knowledge, and research. The information in this book serves as a general guide only. The author and publisher have used their best efforts in preparing this book and disclaim liability rising directly or indirectly from the use and application of this book.

CPSIA Compliance Information: Batch #WS14CSQ

All websites were available and accurate when this book was sent to press.

Library of Congress Cataloging-in-Publication Data
Phillips, H.
Inside a sprint car / by H. Phillips.
p. cm. — (Life in the fast lane)
Includes index.
ISBN 978-1-62713-052-3 (hardcover) ISBN 978-1-62713-054-7 (ebook)
1. Sprint cars — Juvenile literature. 2. Automobile racing — Juvenile literature. I. Phillips, H. II. Title.
GV1029.9.S67 P45 2015
796.72—d23

Editorial Director: Dean Miller
Art Director: Jeffrey Talbot
Production Manager: Jennifer Ryder-Talbot
Production Editor: David McNamara

Packaged for Cavendish Square Publishing, LLC by BlueAppleWorks Inc.
Managing Editor: Melissa McClellan
Designer: Tibor Choleva
Photo Research: Joshua Avramson, Jane Reid
Copy Editor: Catherine Collison, Janis Campbell

The photographs in this book are used by permission and through the courtesy of: Cover photo © John Berry/ Syracuse Newspapers/The Image Works; p. 4, 10, 24–25, 36–37, 39, 41 © David Hill; p. 6, 11, 13, 14–15, 28, 38 © Dale Calnan/ImageFactor.ca; p. 8–9 © John Chapman/Creative Commons; p. 17, 22 john j. klaiber jr/ Shutterstock.com; p. 18 Library of Congress/Public Domain; p. 20 © Daniel Gangur/Shutterstock.com; p. 27 © Ted Van Pelt/Creative Commons; p. 28 top, left to right, © Daniel Raustadt/Dreamstime.com, © Carey Akin/ Creative Commons, © Farrukh/Creative Commons; p. 31 © Jerry Coli/Dreamstime.com; p. 33, 33 inset © Beelde Photography/Shutterstock.com; p. 34 © Doug James/Shutterstock.com

Printed in the United States of America

CONTENTS

Sprint cars zip, slide, and roar around the track.

INTRODUCTION

Imagine yourself behind the wheel of a sprint car! You can taste the dirt from the track in your mouth. You grip the wheel hard as you round the corner. Your back tires start to spin out. The force from the turn knocks your helmet against the **roll bar**. Instead of panicking, you hit the gas and blow past the competition. The wind cools you off as your car thunders down the final stretch with top speeds often exceeding 120 miles per hour (193 km/h). The competitors are gaining. One last burst of speed and the checkered flag drops. The victory is yours.

Sprint cars are small, but they do pack a lot of power. Sprint cars race on short, oval dirt tracks. Fans sit close to the action as the cars zip around the track. Sprint cars slide sideways into turns and come out of them with roaring engines. To some fans, this is the best auto racing. Fasten your seat belts and take a ride into the exciting world of sprint car racing.

The open wheels make a sprint car look like a dune buggy, but it's built for speed and power.

1 THE DIRT ON SPRINT CARS

So what are sprint cars? Even if you are a fan of **NASCAR** or Formula 1, sprint cars may be new to you. While they look more like go-karts or dune buggies, these small **open-wheel cars** can travel fast thanks to their powerful engines. Sprint cars often have **wings** on top of their vehicles, a large one over the back and a smaller one in front. Stranger still, sprint cars have two different-sized tires, with the pair in the back much larger than the front wheels. But all these oddities make sprint cars exciting racecars, combining speed and power.

You won't spot a sprint car on the road. Sprint cars have been designed for racing from the very start. There is no luxury-model sprint car. They don't have cup holders, or sound systems. They have all the right parts for racing, though.

Early sprint cars like this one have the same narrow shape as today's models.

The Body: Small and Mighty

If any part of the sprint car has kept its shape over the years, it is the body. The outer shells of today's sprint cars are shaped the same as the shell of a sprint car of the 1920s.

There are two parts to a sprint car's body: the frame and the outer shell. The frame is the sprint car's skeleton. It connects all the

parts of the car. It holds everything
together and protects both the
driver and the engine during a crash.
The frame is made of metal tubing that
is welded together to form the basic
car shape.

The outer shell is long and narrow. The
shells give sprint cars their shape. Sprint car

Today's sprint cars are required to have a strong steel frame to protect drivers in a crash.

shells are made of **fiberglass**, sheet metal, or aluminum. Fiberglass is stronger and lighter than sheet metal, but it is more expensive. Most sprint cars are from 9 to 10 feet (2.7 to 3 m) long. They cannot be wider than 4 feet (1.2 m). Sprint car officials measure each car before every race. Officials measure the cars so that regulations are followed for each category. Cars that do not measure to the rules are disqualified.

A driver sits in the **cockpit**. A metal cage called a roll bar surrounds the cockpit.

It protects the driver during a crash. Drivers sit near the back of the car. Their feet are just inches from the engine. The car itself is low to the ground. This gives you an idea of just how tiny these race cars really are!

The Engine: Lightning Fast

All sprint cars have eight-cylinder engines. Sprint car engines sit toward the front of the car. Sprint car engines are all about power. Unlike the sprint car body, the sprint car engine has changed dramatically over the years. Today's sprint car engines are

Because a sprint car is small, the driver's feet are just inches away from the powerful engine.

so advanced that they can run up to 800 **horsepower**. This is more than five times as powerful as the engines in cars you see on the street.

There are two sizes of sprint car engines. A sprint car's engine size determines in which class it can race. Most sprint cars use a 360-cubic-inch (5.9-liter) engine. This engine produces up to 750 horsepower. "Outlaw" sprint cars, which race in their own separate division, use 410-cubic-inch (6.7-liter) engines. These engines produce horsepower of 800 or more.

One of the things that makes sprint cars so fast is their light weight. Most sprint cars weigh only 1,300 pounds (590 kg). With a 750- or an 800-horsepower engine, it's no wonder these cars sometimes fly off the track.

The Tires: Dirt Grippers

Terrific tires are important equipment on every car, but especially on race cars. A car can only go as fast as its tires allow. A car can stay on a track as long as its tires have grip that can hold it to the ground against the speed of the car.

Giant rear tires help to control the engine's power.

Sprint cars use extra-wide, treaded tires to keep them on the track. The rear wheels of a sprint car are always wider and larger than the front wheels. Some rear wheels are 20 inches (51 cm) wide. All sprint cars have **rear-wheel drive**. The back tires are large and wide to help control the engine's power. Larger tires help transfer engine power to speed on the track. The smaller front tires help with steering.

Winging It

Sprint cars not only seem to fly down the track, they actually have wings. Most sprint cars have both front and rear wings. Only a few sprint car racing associations don't allow wings.

There is no mistaking a winged sprint car. The wing is half as big as the car itself. A winged sprint car looks as if it might lift

Wings actually help sprint cars stick to the ground. They also act as a crumple zone, protecting the driver if a car does roll over.

off the ground if it were to go fast enough. Actually, the opposite is true.

A big wing sits on top of the car and a smaller wing sits on the front hood. The front of each wing is pointed downward. As the car races around the track, air flows over the wings. The force of the air moving over the wings pushes the car against the ground. This makes the car heavier. A heavier car sticks to the ground better.

A sprint car that sticks to the ground can go faster around a track without spinning out or flipping. Drivers who figure out the best wing position can give their race cars greater speed.

Some drivers and fans prefer wingless racing. Without the advantages and stability the wing provides, it is more difficult to keep control of a sprint car as it gains speed. Vehicles are more likely to slip. This additional challenge adds to the excitement of the race. Luckily, fans don't need to pick one or the other—they can enjoy both styles of sprint car racing.

FAST FACTS

Sprint cars look like miniature works of art. Not only do they have **sponsor** decals, but there are colorful graphics on the little race cars. Entire businesses are devoted to detailing sprint cars. Fans also get in on the action, often wearing shirts or hats with their favorite drivers or teams emblazoned on them.

Before the 1970s, sprint cars did not have wings. Some races today still use wingless sprint cars.

Since the invention of cars, people have loved to go out and watch them race.

Fans are proud of the sprint car racing legacy. According to some historians, the first so-called sprint car race took place in 1896 in Cranston, Rhode Island. Of course, these cars looked much different. But the race was held on an oval track and all the competitors drove small, open-wheel race cars.

In the early part of the 20th century, all kinds of auto racing drew fans and competitors eager to get involved with this new sport. Besides sprint cars, there were speedsters, midgets, big cars, and the even larger championship cars. The only problem was that there weren't many places to race. No one was too eager to build a large, expensive racetrack. What if auto racing was only a fad? Instead of risking big dollars, promoters figured out a better idea. They began running **motor sport** competitions on horse racing tracks.

Sprint cars racing at Rosedale Speedway in Victoria, Australia. Associations dedicated to the sport of sprint car racing can be found all over the world.

Eventually, automobile racing became more popular than the horse races. New tracks began to pop up in several parts of the country. Sprint car racing was not even twenty years old before people began to organize racing associations. These associations would help make sprint car races bigger, better, and more available to the public. The American Automobile Association (AAA) was the first organization to support sprint car events.

In 1915, the International Motor Contest Association (IMCA) was formed. Unlike the AAA, the IMCA focused specifically on auto racing. More associations were formed several years later. There was the American Racing Association (ARA), the Central States Racing Association (CSRA), and the United States Auto Club (USAC). Even NASCAR, the world-famous stock car organization, was involved for two years in sprint car racing.

These days, there are several associations and clubs that are dedicated to the sport of sprint car racing. Among these are the American Sprint Car Series (ASCS) and the World of Outlaws. Outlaws? That name sure doesn't sound like it describes race car drivers or motor sports. But the World of Outlaws is a huge part of the world of sprint car racing.

FAST FACTS

Sprint car racing is a global phenomenon, popular throughout the world. In addition to the United States, sprint car fans can enjoy races in Canada, Europe, Australia, Africa, and many other locations.

A World of Outlaws custom-made car has large adjustable wings and a bigger engine.

I n this case, an outlaw is not a bad guy character in an old Western. In sprint car racing, **outlaw** drivers are not part of a large team—they own their own cars, and make their own decisions.

An outlaw doesn't get the privileges that a team member gets. Outlaws must pay for their own sprint cars. Sometimes an outlaw both builds and drives a sprint car. Most outlaw drivers are also part of their **pit crews**. It is not uncommon to see drivers jump out of the car's cockpit and start working underneath the hood.

In 1978, a man named Ted Johnson had the brilliant idea of gathering all the outlaws and forming them into a group. Johnson organized these free-spirited drivers into the World of Outlaws (WoO). The WoO is now the most famous group of sprint car racers in the country.

It's hard to tell why the World of Outlaws became so popular. It is a combination of

The World of Outlaws really took off after being organized in 1978. It's now the most famous series of sprint car races.

factors. One reason might be the name itself. The World of Outlaws suggests fun and a little bit of danger. People were curious so they first came to these races to see what the excitement was all about.

Another key to the success of the World of Outlaws was the dominating presence of drivers such as Steve Kinser. He is still considered the king of the outlaws.

As of the start of the 2014 racing season he has been the World of Outlaws series champion 20 times, winning more than 500 career WoO A-Feature races in his more than 30-year career.

Finally, the World of Outlaws gets much more **exposure** than any other sprint car association. One reason is that outlaws travel all over the country. Some sprint car racing **circuits** only race in one state or a few states within a region of the country. The World of Outlaws competes all across the United States. Outlaw exposure comes from television, as well. Although most sprint car racing associations cannot be seen on TV, many of the Outlaw races are shown on cable sports networks during the racing season. There are no bad guys, but plenty of good racing excitement when it comes to the World of Outlaws.

FAST FACTS

Steve Kinser is the rock star of sprint car racing, with more than 800 career victories! Many people attribute the rise in sprint car popularity solely to Steve. He's also a winning family man, with his wife, Dana, cheering him on, and their three grown children also following in their dad's tracks and interests. Daughter Stevie is involved in the family racing business, and son Kraig is a member of Tony Stewart's World of Outlaws racing team. Another son, Kurt, is now a mixed martial arts (MMA) fighter.

Steve Kinser has won 20 World of Outlaws national titles, including in 1986, when this photo was taken.

A. J. Foyt

Jack Hewitt

Bobby Unser

Sprint car racing has been a training ground for future NASCAR, Formula 1, and Indy car champions.

I f you're a fan of motor sports, chances are you'll know these names: Mario Andretti, A. J. Foyt, Jeff Gordon, Jack Hewitt, and Bobby Unser. Even casual racing fans will recognize a few of these names.

Jeff Gordon has been the top NASCAR driver for a number of years. Back in 1995, Jeff was voted the Winston Cup Rookie of the Year. The following year, he won the Winston Cup title. Like many auto racers, Jeff Gordon got his start on sprint car tracks. Sprint car tires were his training wheels. He's been competing and winning ever since.

It's the same story with the other four drivers. They all started out racing open-wheel sprinters before moving on to different kinds of racing.

Jack Hewitt set a racing record that still stands on September 26, 1998, at Eldora Speedway in Ohio. He won nationals in four categories: sprints, midgets, dirt champ cars, and modifieds. Now retired, he finished his career with 46 sprint car wins and many other victories.

A. J. Foyt drove lots of different kinds of race cars. A. J. was a great sprint car driver. He won many races during the early 1960s. After 1964, A. J. moved from sprint car racing to Indy car racing. He won the Indianapolis 500 four times during his career.

Mario Andretti is a huge name in motor sports. Mario's career started on the dirt tracks of the sprint car circuit at about the same time as A. J. Foyt's. He also moved on and up to race Indy cars after a few years. Later in his career, he moved to the international Formula 1 circuit. He was the world champion Formula 1 racer in 1977.

Bobby Unser is considered one of the best Indy car drivers of all time. He won the Indianapolis 500 three times. Bobby was just as impressive when he was a sprint car racer in the 1960s. He often went on long consecutive winning streaks. Nobody drove faster.

For these drivers, and many others that made the move to different racing circuits, sprint car racing was a favorite time of their careers. Most sprint car drivers love the competitive races and the intimate tracks.

Mario Andretti became a racing legend after coming to the U.S. from Italy at age 15. He won 111 races in sprint cars, Formula 1 cars, and stock cars.

Sprint cars taught them how to be great drivers, and they applied these lessons in other styles of racing. Other sprint car racers love it so much, they never leave the circuit, choosing to remain on the dirt tracks.

FAST FACTS

To say NASCAR superstar Jeff Gordon has been driving most of his life is no exaggeration. When he was just 5 years old, his stepdad gave him a quarter midget race car and it was love at first lap! On his web site, www.jeffgordon.com, his family shares that he was practicing lap after lap, pretty much every night from that day on. He won his first quarter midget championship when he was 8. Jeff continued racing and winning, and after a few years, the family decided to leave California for better racing competition and opportunities. They moved to Florida and then settled in Indiana where Jeff could race sprint cars with his parents' permission. And race he did, winning three sprint car championships before he was even old enough to get his driver's license!

Jeff Gordon greets race fans. Before he was a NASCAR star, he won sprint car races as a teen.

Crew members unload the sprint cars from the trucks and get them ready for a race.

Are you ready for the races? Because most sprint car tracks are dirt and not all that big, there are a lot of tracks around the country. Sprint car races take place all across the United States each week. There's sprint car racing all year, so even when it's not in your area, you can follow the results online.

A few thousand people pack the speedway stands to watch the races. Some of the championship races, such as the Knoxville Nationals in Iowa, can draw much larger crowds.

It's easy for your family and friends to plan a day or an evening at the racetrack. Compared to professional sporting events or even college athletics, tickets for sprint car races are very affordable.

At some races, fans can also buy special passes to visit the pit area, see the cars, take photos, and get autographs.

A special helmet, fire-retardant suit, and head surround with shoulder support built into the seat are part of a sprint car driver's safety equipment.

The Racing Circuit

Racing organizations sponsor sprint car races. There are more than 30 different sprint car racing organizations. Many of these associations sponsor races locally or within a state. Several organizations sponsor races that take place at different racetracks around the country.

Sprint car racers race on a circuit. They may race every week at different tracks or at the same track. Each racer wins points for finishing a race. The more points racers get

at the finish, the more points they earn toward the season championship.

A season could be ten, or even twenty, races. The racer with the most points at the end of the season is crowned the series champion.

On the Fast Track

All sprint car races are held on oval tracks. Most sprint car tracks are made of packed dirt, but some tracks are made of asphalt.

Sprint car tracks are not always the same length. Some tracks are three-eighths

Workers groom a sprint car track before a race. Most tracks are made of packed dirt.

of a mile (0.6 km). Others are one-third of a mile (0.5 km). Some oval tracks are one-half of a mile long (0.8 km). The length of the track affects a sprint car's speed and the driver's strategy.

Sprint cars race down the **straightaway** at almost 120 miles per hour (193 km/h)! The racers must slow down quickly at turns. They often send their cars into a sideways slide at about 90 miles per hour (145 km/h). As the cars come out of the turn, their engines roar and send them speeding down the track to the next turn. Some tracks are specially built to allow sprint cars go even faster. Reaching speeds over 140 miles per hour (225 km/h) is possible on such tracks.

The action on the track is always fast and furious. Cars bunch together in the turns. They knock wheels and butt fenders. Some-times the wheels get locked together and send the cars spinning into the walls.

Plenty of Heats

Sometimes 30 sprint cars or more enter a racing event. There could be only one race

Sprint cars don't turn on with a key like a regular car. Another car, called a push car, gives a push from behind to get a sprint car started.

staged, but then it would last less than one hour. To make the excitement last, shorter **heat** races are run. Heat races determine which racers get into the main event and race for the event championship.

For most sprint car circuits, heat races are ten laps around the oval track. The number of cars entered in a race determines how many heats are run and how many cars race in each heat. Twenty-eight or more cars will race in four heats and a semifinal. Each heat will have six or seven cars. Five racers from each heat will move on to the semifinals or finals.

The final race to determine the event champion is raced by twenty-four or twenty-five racers. Final races are usually thirty laps around the oval. The sprint cars line up side-by-side in rows of two. Sprint car races have a running start. The cars run around the track and wait for the green flag. When the cars are even as they come to the line, the green flag starts the race. Engines scream, dirt flies, and the fans cheer wildly for their favorite racers.

What a finish! Fans—dusty and hoarse from cheering—have had a long day or night at the track, but they'll be back!

Knoxville Raceway in Iowa calls itself the "Sprint Car Capital of the World."

FAST FACTS

Dirt-track racing stays true to its roots at historic Knoxville Raceway near Des Moines, Iowa. Sprint cars race on black Iowa soil at Knoxville, just as horses once did. Knoxville, which was built in the 1880s, hosted its first car race in 1901 and began offering a full season of sprint car racing in 1954. More than 270,000 fans from all over the world come to the races each year, especially for the Knoxville Nationals in August. Knoxville calls itself the Sprint Car Capital of the World and is also home to the growing National Sprint Car Museum and Hall of Fame.

WORDS TO KNOW

circuit: a series of organized races

cockpit: the part of a sprint car where the driver sits

exposure: notice or attention

fiberglass: a material that is stronger and lighter than sheet metal

heat: an early race held to determine which drivers advance in a competition

horsepower: a unit to measure the power of engines

motor sport: any competition involving automobiles of any kind

NASCAR: stands for the National Association for Stock Car Auto Racing

open-wheel car: any race car on which the wheels are not covered by the car's frame or body

outlaw: a sprint car driver who is not sponsored by a team

pit crews: the team of people that service or work on the car during the race

rear-wheel drive: a transmission system that provides power to the rear wheels of a motor vehicle. All sprint cars have rear-wheel drive

roll bar: a strong cage made of steel that helps to protect a driver during a crash

sponsor: a company that pays a racer to advertise its products, usually by placing their logos or brand names on the racer's clothing, gear, or car. Sponsors also pay money to sponsor racing events

straightaway: the long sections of the racetrack

wing: a part attached to a sprint car that forces air onto the car to hold the car on the racetrack at high speeds

FURTHER READING

Books

Sprint Cars
Tyrone Georgiou
New York, NY
Gareth Stevens Publishing
2011

Sprint Cars
Sarah L. Schuette
Mankato, MN
Blazers
2006

Sprint Cars
Denny Von Finn
Minneapolis, MN
Bellwether Media
2009

Websites

Knoxville Raceway
www.knoxvilleraceway.com
Fans can find weekly photos and
information about their favorite drivers.

National Sprint Car Hall of Fame and Museum
www.sprintcarhof.com
This website has biographies of the Hall of
Fame sprint car racers as well as a virtual
tour of photos of cars and drivers.

Ohsweken Speedway
www.ohswekenspeedway.ca
A popular raceway in Canada is an excellent
site to explore the Canadian racers'
information and schedule.

World of Outlaws
www.woosprint.com
This site features schedules, results, photos,
and videos of the World of Outlaws circuit.

RESOURCES

Organizations

International Motor Contest Association
1800 W D St.
Vinton, IA 52349
www.imca.com

National Championship Racing Association
7700 N. Broadway
Wichita, KS 67219
www.racencra.com

INDEX

About the Author

H. Phillips is a racing enthusiast who lives in Indiana, where he has attended the famed Indy 500 for years. A native of upstate New York, H. spent his teenage years racing dirt bikes through back roads.